The National Tramway Museum

In the beginning there was no time and no place. Just men with a mission and a desperate desire to rescue, store and restore as many trams as possible during the "Termination Terror" of the 1950's.

Truly men of vision – for the trams return. By stealth or with a fanfare, trams are coming back on track – but those at the National Tramway Museum are the originals!

This award winning "Museum on the Move" has gradually been developed to become one of the finest transport Museums in the country, and if you haven't visited for several years – you must! It's a continually changing and ever-fascinating place.

The National Tramway Museum, Crich, Derbyshire. Tel: 01773 852565

This edition first published 1995 by Milepost Publishing in conjunction with
Arcturus Publishing Limited and exclusively for Bookmart Limited
Desford Road, Enderby, Leicester, LE9 5AD

Milepost Publishing is a division of Milepost 92^1/$_2$,
Colin Garratt's Audio Visual, Photographic and Picture Library for the Railway Industry

Designed by Milepost/Wilson Design Associates
Originated, Printed and Bound in the UK by Gresham Print Group, Nottingham

ISBN 1 900193 15 9

Milepost 92^1/$_2$
Newton Harcourt
Leicestershire
LE8 9FH
Tel:0 0116 259 2068

MILEPOST

TRAMS
OF NORTHERN BRITAIN

MILEPOST

INTRODUCTION

The light, the landscapes and the industries provide the Northern settings for Henry Priestley's tramway photographs. Canaletto would have refused to paint in the Northern mists, but this is Laurence Lowry country. The grime of industry and a myriad domestic coal fires darkened the buildings; apart from a few signs and advertisements, the tram was often the only splash of colour in an urban scene.

Henry Priestley travelled widely to record tramway images. One week in 1954 found him on successive days in Glasgow, Aberdeen, Edinburgh and Liverpool. And what a variety to see! Tramway reserved sleeper tracks to new estates formed part of urban planning in Liverpool and Leeds; by contrast, trams and tracks were squeezed into narrow streets in Dundee.

It was a world less sophisticated than today, where a tram ride to the park was an afternoon out, and most shops were locally owned. Only in a few late shots do self-service appear, and the hypermarket is as far away in the future as the personal computer.

Henry Priestley records these vistas on a wide screen, and if you are tempted to step into them and explore, why not? The Past may be a far country, but always worth a visit.

Dublin was different. The front balcony of a Dublin United car gives a view from Dalkey Depot of the Irish standard 5ft 3in gauge track, even more impressive in the street than on the main line railways. And how that wall on the right must have thrown back the echoes as the car ahead pulled away!

Previous spread
To save the cost of renewing tram tracks, many towns in the 1930's changed to trolleybuses. On 25 June 1938 Henry Priestley parked his motorbike JP 364 at Dod-Lea to record 18- year old Huddersfield balcony car 120. Already the extra wires are in place for trolleybuses, and the conductor has his bamboo pole hooked over the trolley pole, ready to turn it for the journey back to town.

City centres in the 1950's, smoky grey and granite, before the motor car took over.
Top left in Leeds contrasts a 1930-built ex-London car with a 1926 Leeds design; *Below left and top right* are examples of Leeds 1931 Horsfield styling, while *below right* is one of Aberdeen's 1949 centre entrance cars.

The sheer emptiness of roads, still possible in Leeds, *above left,* where blue liveried Horsfield car 160 sails past railway posters in Marsh Lane in May, 1939, possible too in August that year in Gateshead, *below left,* where children cross unworried by single deck front exit car 16 as it emerges from Sunderland Road depot. And still to be found in Sheffield in 1952, *above,* where 1935-built standard car 226's cream and blue paintwork glistens among the grime of the steelworks. The long shelters house queues of workers at shift-change times; a line of six trams could move 500 people.

Over page
Another photographer might have moved the wheelbarrow and tidied the clutter, or chosen another angle to record this depot interior in Halifax. But Henry Priestley gives it all, the basic maintenance facilities that ensured that these sturdy and comfortable 3ft 6in gauge cars climbed safely up and down in a town with scarcely more than a few yards of level track. This is one of the earliest shots in this book, taken two days before Christmas, 1936.

View from a tram top as ex-London Feltham 534 and a 1920's Chamberlain car approach with Leeds Parish Church as a backdrop.

Two of Glasgow's much-rebuilt standard cars in George Square, in 1954, car 186 dates from 1913, rebuilt in 1930.

Dundee, like Glasgow and Leeds, changed from trolley pole to bow collector. Car 38, seen in 1955, dates from 1921.

Liverpool used trolley poles to the end. 1937-built car 938 passes Coronation decorations in Parker Street, June 1953.

Many-textured road surfaces, uncluttered by motor traffic. 1932-style Edinburgh car 180 reverses at Merchiston siding, *left*, watched by a crew with summer white tops to their hats in July 1955. *Above*, Two Leeds Chamberlain design cars of 1926/27 in full pre-war blue livery at Balm Road terminus in May 1939. Cigarettes advertised freely and Alexander's Ragtime Band at the Strand Cinema.

Rain and poor light call forth the photographer's skill. Two views of Sunderland on 30 October 1953 show, *below left*, a much rebuilt 1903 car, no. 63 at Derwent Street, little more than a dark reflection on the glistening setts, and, *above*, car 24 at Fulwell on smooth tarmacadam paved track. This car was built in 1933 using the body of a Mansfield tram; in all Sunderland collected second-hand bargains from eight towns. In Sheffield, *top left*, 1921-built car 382 turns right at Hunter's Bar while an RAC motorcycle patrolman waits for passengers to board car 247, beyond.

Whether following the road or cutting across country, reserved tracks gave trams a chance to show their speed and cost less to build than paved street tracks. These examples in Leeds are at Roundhay Park, *top* and *below, left*, and in Middleton Woods, above. The Middleton light railway left the roads completely to provide a direct route to a large housing estate. Leeds Horsfield tramcars are at home in these surroundings, yet what a contrast with city streets!

Smoke still pours out of a works chimney in aptly named Vulcan Road, Sheffield, on Palm Sunday, 1958, while another photographer records the tram used by Henry Priestley to capture the scene, *left*, now deserted, but thronged at every shift change. *Above* the water tower of Walton prison forms a grim backdrop in February 1955 to 1937-built Liverpool streamline car 166.

The broad view at Cabin station in August 1958, where Blackpool's tramroad to Fleetwood, *top left*, displays tramcars dating from 1928 to 1953; a similar view of Blackpool's promenade at Foxhall out of season in April 1953, *bottom left*, shows English Electric railcoaches of 1934 in two paint-styles. English Electric also built Bradford car 257 in 1919, seen with others, *centre left*, outside Thornbury Depot in July 1939. Suburban and city settings *this page* for Sheffield tramcars 222 of 1935 at Handsworth in 1930 and 126 of 1923 using the trolley reverser at Suffolk Street in 1952. Will the man in a motorised invalid carriage catch up with the tram?

Trams in light traffic at Shore Road, Belfast with former horse tram 244 doing snowplough duty in 1951, *top*; Car 132 of 1910, now preserved, passes Cottingham Road, Hull in 1938, *above*; Forster Square, Bradford with car 241 in 1938, *top right*; and Marsh Lane/York Street junction, Leeds with blue liveried 1931 Horsfield car 239 in May 1939.

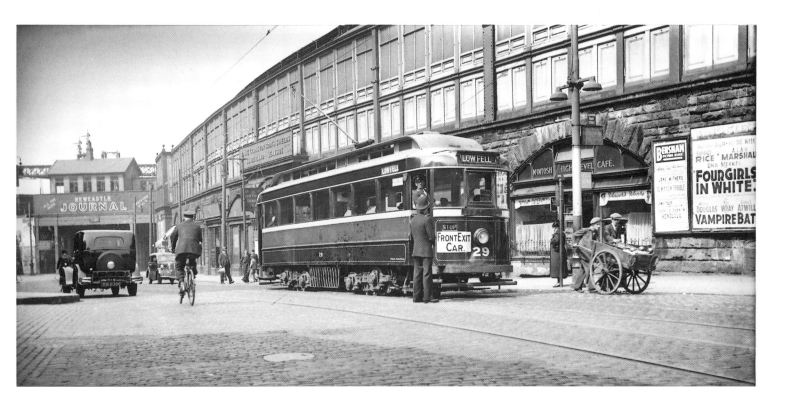

Like Bradford, Blackburn used four foot gauge track. Its cars were solid, foursquare in dark green and ivory. *Left*, car 65, a 1920's rebuild of a 1900 Milnes product, stands among Blackburn and Ribble buses at the Railway Station in April 1939. Much rebuilt also is Newcastle car 29 at Gateshead station in August 1939 *top right*; and *below right* Liverpool 944, built only the previous year, shows off the pre-war olive green livery at Lodge Lane junction in May 1938.

Previous spread
Camera held firmly against the bulkhead door, Henry Priestley captures Sheffield 1933-built car 132, still in the old dark blue livery, as it heads from Abbey Lane towards the city across the junction with the Meadowhead route. The driver has stood aside to reveal his controller, left, and the hand brake handle and track brake wheel, right.

A tram under a bridge is an actor on a stage. Oldfield Lane bridge sets the scene for blue-liveried Leeds Horsfield 204 in March 1938, *top left*; while red-painted car 167 passes a parade of pre-war petrol pumps near Burley Road bridge in April 1954 *below*. In the same year in Liverpool, Walton station bridge, *above*, carries a co-op advert with strong echoes of 1951 Festival of Britain styling; the tram underneath dates from 1937.

Horse-drawn vehicles figure strongly here, a Clydesdale heavy horse pulls a lurry past ex-Manchester car 48 of 1930-32 at Queen's Cross depot junction, Aberdeen in 1954 *top left*, while *below left* a rag and bone man leads his pony off the tram tracks as Manchester 1927-built car 1009 loads passengers at Hulme Church in August 1938, a scene now dominated by the Chester Road flyover, whilst *above*, a Shire heavy draught horse pulls a heavy cart full of builder's material at the Park Avenue/Laisteridge Lane junction in Bradford. The tram dates from 1920, the date is Saturday 2 July 1938, and Bradford City's football ground is just down the road.

Take the tram to the corner shop, for aniseed cough balsam at Compton Road terminus Leeds, *bottom left*, where Chamberlain car 443 in March 1938 has yet to exchange its trolleypole for a bow collector, or for White Rose Oil or an Echo radio at Tottington terminus, Bury, *top left*, in April 1937, where 1926-built car 57 has just arrived. Or visit the pawnbrokers and outfitters on Wakefield Road, Bradford, *above*, where car 31 takes power from the positive trolleybus wire as it climbs the hill.

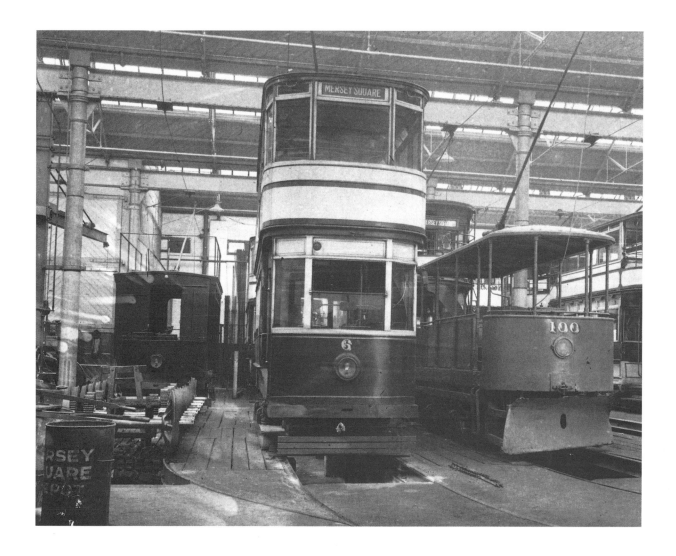

The tram indoors, in depots and repair workshops, in 1937 at Dundee's Lochee depot *top left*, in 1936 at Stockport Mersey Square *top right*, in 1938 at Bradford's Thornbury depot *bottom left*, and in 1954 in Kirkstall Road works, Leeds, *bottom right*. The Bradford line-up is not quite what it seems; all these cars have been given new numbers to avoid awkward questions about a batch of cars with poor bodywork which had to be scrapped early.

Crowds spilling off the pavements, in St Nicholas Street, Aberdeen, *left*, where olive green painted car 105, rugged and sturdy, swings from single track into a passing loop in August 1955. At Blackburn in April 1939, *top right*, Milnes bogie car 62 heads for Preston New Road past Woolworth's 3d and 6d Stores at Salford junctions, and wide-bodied Lochee car 24 takes the centre track in Dundee High Street in August 1955, *bottom right*.

Trams and urchins in Liverpool: Both pictures were taken on 16 October 1954, with 1937-built streamline car 962 at Everton road junction, *left*, and sister-car 963 at the corner of Eastbourne Street and Fitzclarence Street. How those large cars swept around the sinuous curves between the soot-grimed buildings! Overhead wiring above 963 has already been prepared for the change to bow collectors which never took place in Liverpool.

Over page
The lower end of the Middleton reserved track light railway in Leeds ran through industrial wasteland landscapes. Children carry jars indicating a visit to Parkside newt ponds nearby. Car 257, in the distance, is one of those built specially for this route in 1935.

Child's eye view of trams. In Leeds, *top left*, car 151 still with a trolleypole in March 1938, pauses at the Barley Mow loop, Bramley. In Manchester, car 357 is about to turn from Princess Road into Denmark Road in August 1938, *bottom left*, car 1017 is followed by a heavily-laden lorry out of Booth Street West, *this page, top*, and people cross casually behind car 876 at Miles Platting, *this page, bottom*, while Heginbottom's tripe works' van pushes ahead.

Two streets, both with tramtracks: *Above*, Car 1024 was built by Liverpool in 1936 and came to Glasgow in February 1954; two months later Henry Priestley saw it at St George's Cross. The Yorkshire Penny Bank marks the corner at Kirkgate, Leeds, in May 1939, *top right*, and by this time all Leeds cars, like 125 here, carry bow collectors. By 1954, television aerials have begun to sprout at Abbey Hill, Edinburgh, *bottom right*, where the traffic policeman has just waved 1936-built car 45 on its way, though his duties do not seem otherwise too demanding.

Trams on the Irish broad gauge: Dublin United Tramways built car 287 in 1927, and, *above*, it pauses outside Harcourt Street Station in April 1939. Even after Dublin's last tram ran in 1949, the Great Northern Railway (Ireland) continued to run its Hill of Howth tramway; in August 1956, *right*, car 6 of the original 1900 batch waits at Howth Station for the run to Sutton. Track is laid GNR(I) fashion with bullhead rail, keyed inside so that one platelayer can check both rails at once.

The textured road surface of setts and tram rails fascinated Henry Priestley at Liverpool, *above*, where car 948 prepares to round the curve at Aubrey Street in October 1954, and in Leeds at Balm Road Mills in May 1939, *top right*, where the single track section shows an obvious candidate for road widening. The factory chimney overshadows the line of washing behind the houses. Rain in Sunderland in October 1953 gives reflections of car 24, rebuilt in 1933 from a Mansfield tramcar, *bottom right*. The track to the right leads to the football ground.

Classic Henry Priestley planning for this top deck view of Leeds 176 at Rookwood, *above*, taken in August 1959. Careful composition too at Sea Beach, Aberdeen, *top right*, where the long queue barriers speak of summer crowds, though only a few will board post-war centre entrance car 39 on this August day in 1955. Tramway extension and new estates went together in Leeds, *bottom right*, with ex-London car 549 at Middleton Ring Road.

The date is 2 August 1938 and the photographer's motor-car is legally parked alongside the sign forbidding waiting on odd dates in Brook Street, Manchester, *top left*, as 1928-built car 352 approaches the Grosvenor Street junction. The same motor-car appears, *above*, at Westhoughton terminus in April 1938, where Bolton tramcar 99, much rebuilt from a 1910 model, boldly displays route letter E. Somewhat grander limousines park in Dublin's O'Connell Street, *bottom left*, in April 1939 while balcony car 289 reverses at Nelson Pillar.

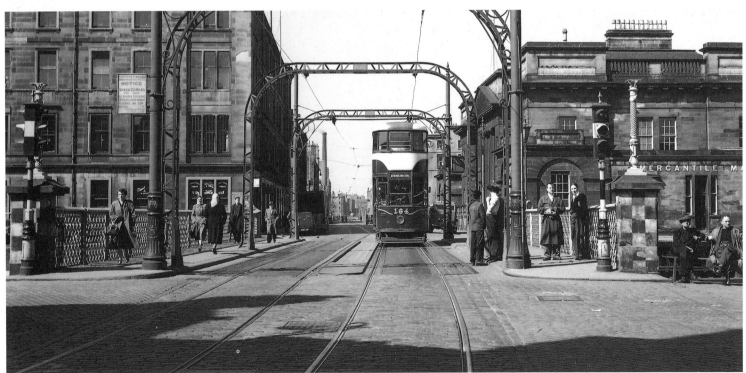

Trams framed by bridges: At Leith Trinity Road, Edinburgh car 304 of 1923 follows an S-shaped course to negotiate the corner in April 1954, *top left*, while 1935 Edinburgh standard car 164 rumbles across Bernard Street swing bridge, *bottom left*. Gateshead car 29, seen in August 1939 beneath Gateshead Station arch, *above*, is a rebuild of an 1899 Liverpool car. The crossover on interlaced track would have caught Henry Priestley's eye.

Over Page
Child's eye view of a holiday town with 1938 fashions, a speeding cyclist, visitors' cars parked, and two tramcars picking up and setting down passengers. The scene is Church Street, Blackpool; balcony cars 146 and 160 date from 1924 and 1927. The Yorkshire Penny Bank has a branch in this Lancashire resort.

City streets, incomplete without tracks and wires. Newcastle's Grainger Street in August 1937 already has a crossing of trolleybus wires, *above*, front-exit tramcar 291 is a standard vehicle of 1921-1926 build. Bradford Forster Square, *top right*, already has some trolleybus wiring in July 1939, car 255 was built as recently as 1930. With Leeds parish church as background in May 1951, *bottom right*, Chamberlain car 131 shows the later blue livery.

One tramcar, two motor-cars, one pedestrian, a motor-cycle combination and a tradesmen's delivery cyclist share Liverpool's Walton Lane on a misty day in April 1954, *top left*, while works car 2 and Lochee car 19 pass in North Tay Street, Dundee in August 1955, *bottom left*. Also in 1955, *above*, Horsfield cars 237 and 247 of 1931/2 reverse at Meanwood Terminus, Leeds, in June sunshine.

These three Edinburgh flat roof standard cars, seen at Goldenacre, *above*, in April 1954, date from 1933 and 1927. In Sheffield, *top right*, car 258 of 1937 waits for car 65 of 1930 to clear the single track at Malin Bridge in June 1938. Some tracks are already tarred over at Brownlow Hill junction, *bottom right*, in May 1955, where Liverpool tramcars 909 and 914, both dating from 1936, look well in post-war livery. Already the international standard No Entry signs have appeared.

The two Bradford trams, *top left*, at the Alhambra in July 1939, are low-height cars for the Greengates route. In the background, right is a single deck trolleybus, on left a two-wheeled horse-drawn cart. *Bottom left*, the slanting sunshine at Swinegate depot entrance, Leeds, picks out details of the track as car 74, now in red livery, heads for Belle Isle. Trackwork details at Govan, Glasgow, show up well as standard car 365, 1930 rebuild of a 1905 vehicle, crosses the junction, *above*.

Suburban sleeper tracks and traffic islands, in Liverpool, *top left*, at Black Horse loop, and at Broad Green Hospital, *top right*, both with 1937-built cars in April 1954; and in the same month at Anniesland, Glasgow, *bottom left*, with standard hex-dash car 154 of 1913. In August 1938, *bottom right*, Salford 348, formerly a front-exit car, is at Irlams o'th' Height terminus.

Tram follows traffic at Garston, Liverpool in April 1952, *above*, while traffic waits for tram to turn left at Upper Brook Street, Manchester in August 1938, *below*. In the far distance, parked beyond the crossing, is the photographer's car.

A passenger alights in the roadway from Liverpool car 986 at Crown Street in April 1954, *above*, and in the same month ex-Liverpool car 1018 approaches St George's Cross, Glasgow, *below*. Massey's on the left already offers self-service, but still does deliveries by bicycle with basket.

Sheffield briefly tried a colour scheme of two shades of green, carried by car 253 on a grey day at Pitsmoor in July 1952, *top left*. The schoolboy, right, has found something far more fascinating! The city quickly returned to the blue and cream colours carried by car 234 at Holme Lane in September 1951, *bottom left*. The quality of Sheffield's asphalt paving shows up, even around depot approach tracks. Another depot approach, *above*, this time sett-paved, is at Queens Road where in October 1957 a zebra crossing has appeared, though tramcar, police box, shelter and street furniture reflect early Sheffield patterns.

Over Page
Sunlight filters down into Langside Depot, Glasgow, in August 1955. Cleaners' galleries, suspended from the roof, dominate the scene. A difficult exposure, so Henry Priestley holds the camera against the bulkhead of standard car 122 to record its controls as well as the standard car, Coronation and works car in one almost cloister-like scene.

Track repairs, at Highfields, Sheffield, in May 1952, *top left*; Edge Lane, Liverpool, in April 1954, *bottom left*; and The Gynn, Blackpool, in April 1952, *above*. This is pick and shovel work, only one pneumatic drill in sight. No traffic cones, safety helmets, or high visibility clothing. Sheffield and Liverpool scenes show why reserved sleeper track was always cheaper to build and maintain, there was no road surface to lift before getting at the track

Henry Priestley tried to record textures of road surfaces, buildings, ironwork, along with the trams and the track. In Dundee, *above*, in August 1955 Lochee car 24 approaches track worn below the level of the setts. Outside Anfield Cemetery, Liverpool, *top right*, points are cleaned in April 1954 with no more than a red flag to warn oncoming traffic on the heavily patched road surface. In the same month, *bottom right*, Castle Junction, Aberdeen offers an uncompromising pattern of setts, tracks and granite buildings, with 1949-built car 22 among the sturdy products of the 1920's.

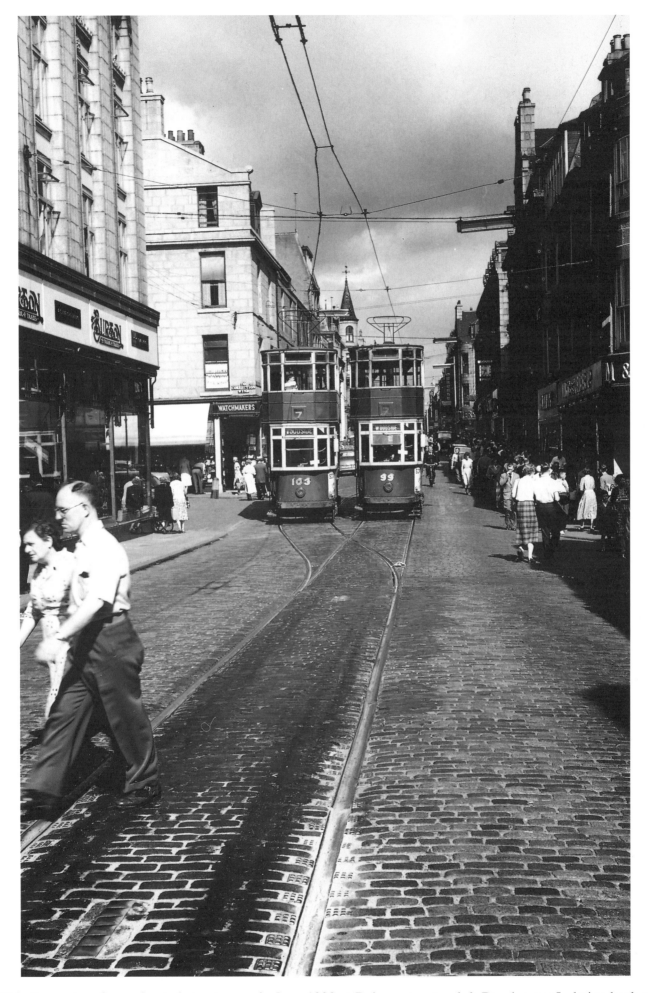

Hull 148 is the centre of an animated street scene in June 1938 at Dairycoates, *top left,* Dundee car 5, dating back to 1900, approaches the West Port/North Tay Street junction in August 1955, *bottom left,* and in the same month two Aberdeen cars pass on one of the St Nicholas Street loops (compare with earlier view), *above.*

Looking down on four foot gauge tracks, from one Bradford balcony to another, car 23 of 1929 on Wibsey Hill at Thornton Lane, *above*, in July 1938, and at Blackburn car 45, rebuilt in the 1920's from 1900 open top, *below*, as it approaches the Darwen boundary in April 1939. The factory chimney showing above the field gives an almost surrealist atmosphere to the scene.